I0187714

HELLO...
CAN YOU HEAR ME?

SHERYL CARPENTER

the book incubator

Sheryl Carpenter

The author and illustrator assert their legal and moral rights. All rights reserved. Apart from fair dealing for the purposes of private study, research, criticism, or review, as permitted under the Copyright Act, no part of this book may be reproduced in any format without the written permission of the author, illustrator and publisher.

Published by the Book Incubator, 2022
www.bookincubator.com.au
Busselton, Western Australia

Hello... Can you hear me? © Sheryl Carpenter
Illustrations ©Kate Heaslip

Book layout and design by The Book Incubator

SBN: 978-0-6454643-8-2

the book
incubator

This book is dedicated to anyone who has experienced a similar situation to my own. I want you to know that you are not alone. There are people who will listen if you can find the courage to give them a chance to hear you.

I hear you.

Warmly,

Sheryl

Sheryl Carpenter

Hello?

Can you hear me?

I need someone to talk to.

Will you listen to my story?

My name is Sheryl.

I am eleven.

Sheryl Carpenter

2

I live right in town and my Nanna lives next door.

Ours is the house with the dead lawn out the front, a wood heap on the side and a mean old dog tied up on a chain.

The dog's name is Billy - but be careful - Billy doesn't like people.

There is no garden at my house but there are lots of wine bottles, beer bottles, cigarette butts and crap everywhere.

Nanna's house is beautiful. Her garden is neat and tidy – just like Nanna.

Everybody in town knows my family. I think some people in town might be scared of us.

It's hard to know.
Not many people talk to me.

In my family there is my mum and my dad, four older brothers, three older sisters, my younger brother, and me. Eleven of us altogether.

My oldest brother died when he was only six. I never knew him but sometimes Mum talks to me about him. It makes her very sad.

Two of my older brothers have already left home.
I wish that they didn't come back to visit.

But they do. Regularly.

I wonder if other kids live the same as me. Are they too embarrassed to have friends visit? Do other kids have friends who are banned from playing at their house? Do other kids live in houses that are filthy, dirty and smelly like mine?

Do other kids go hungry too?

Hello... Can you hear me?

I wish over, and over, and over again that when I am crying or upset at school, that someone would notice me. I wish that someone would listen to what I need to say. I wish that someone would listen to hear me. I wish that someone would show me that they care.

But they don't. And mostly, even if they did, I don't feel safe enough to tell them anyhow. I feel like they probably wouldn't believe me. The other kids seem to know that it is okay to bully me. It's like they know that no one is going to stand up for me. I don't know how they know. I just know. I am alone. I am trying to be strong, but it is hard.

I have never told my teachers what is going on at home. I am embarrassed. I am ashamed and I feel all alone.

At school, the teachers tell us kids to speak up and let our parents know if someone treats us badly. But what if the bad stuff is happening at home? And, what if you do speak up and no one listens? I told Mum that my older brothers come into my room at night. I told her what they do. She called me names. She told me I was a lying little bitch. She ranted and raved. She told me I was always trying to get the boys into trouble.

I never told her anything again.

Hello... Can you hear me?

I want to tell my mum what happens when she sends me to
the pub to buy her the plonk she so desperately wants.
I want to tell her, but I think she already knows.
I want to scream, "Mum! How can you let this happen?"

But I don't.

I don't say anything. I know she won't listen.
Besides, I'm sure that sometimes the plonk is more
important to her than I am.

I wonder what it would be like if
Mum didn't start drinking before breakfast.
Would she help me with my homework?
Would she walk me to school?
Would she take pride in our home or the garden
or maybe even do the laundry once in a while?
Would she have time for me?

Sometimes I wonder what life must feel like for my mum.
Mum had nine kids. Somehow, while having all those kids it
seems my mum forgot how to take care of herself
and she forgot how to take care of us.
She forgot how to cook and she forgot how to clean.

7

My mum's first baby was born with encephalitis.
Nanna looked after him but Nanna forgot to give
him back and then he died when he was six. I think
Mum is still sad.

I wonder what it would be like if my dad didn't drink
all the time. He leaves work and goes straight to the
pub and doesn't come home until the pub closes.
When he does come home he is drunk and he is
angry. He argues and fights with my brothers. It is
scary. If Dad wasn't drunk all the time, I wonder
what he would be like as a father. Would he
protect me? He sure doesn't now - he belts me all
the time. I never ever wonder what life feels like for
my dad. That is strange, isn't it?

Nanna is Dad's mum. She is a God-fearing Baptist
woman. I guess until now I thought life was okay for
Dad when he was a kid, but maybe it wasn't.

I have heard people say that Dad's brothers are
bastards who are all tarred with the same brush. So
maybe there is a lot more underneath all of this that
I do not know about.
It makes me feel sad and scared
to think about that.

Hello... Can you hear me?

I wonder what it is like to have a Christmas tree.
I imagine a beautiful tree with tinsel and bobbles
and gifts underneath!

I imagine people smiling and laughing and having
fun. How magical that would be! I dream that one
day I might receive a present. Even just once.

The other kids talk about presents and how Father
Christmas visits them.

Other kids talk about having roast chook for
Christmas dinner. They talk about their "crazy"
relatives and all the fun that they have. They
don't know it, but those other kids,
they don't truly understand "crazy".

My family is crazy (and not the good kind either),
and we certainly don't have roast chook or
anything else for a special Christmas dinner.
There is no celebration. Nothing.

Father Christmas doesn't visit my family.

Father Christmas doesn't know my address.

Hello... Can you hear me?

Sheryl Carpenter

One time my Nanna hid me when Mum was chasing after me with a whip. Mum was angry with me about something that I had not even done. Mum didn't ask questions, she just pulled out the whip.

Thanks Nanna. I wish you could hide me every day because I get hurt a lot.

I love my friend Leanne. We play together for hours on end. I don't remember when we were not friends. I hope we will be friends forever.

Leanne and I like to just hang out and play. She has a tank stand at her place and we hang upside down by our legs.
We laugh and talk about all sorts of stuff.

One day while we were hanging upside down. I let go of one hand and slipped. I fell into the wooden drain. I was screaming in pain. I broke my arm.
I ran home. Mum and Dad were not there.

Nanna and Uncle Les drove me to the hospital.

Sheryl Carpenter

Hello... Can you hear me?

I love my friend Carol.

We play with her dolls or
we go to the creek and catch tadpoles.

Sometimes I love being eleven!

Sheryl Carpenter

I also love collecting bamboo sticks.
One of my older brothers and I make high jumps from them.
This brother is a safe place for me. He has never hurt me.
We make the stands out of bamboo,
then we put nails going up each side so
we can raise the bar as we get better at jumping.

I love high jumping and I am good at it. I have been
crowned Champion Girl at school more than once.
No one bullies me when I am the sports champion.

Sometimes I wonder how different my life might be
if I came from a different family.

What if my parents weren't alcoholics?
What if i wasn't hurt or beaten?
What if there was enough food to eat?
What if there was clean clothing to wear?
What if I wasn't scared of my family?

Oh my! My life would be very different!

Maybe I will grow up to be a sporting star. One of my
teachers seems to think I can. He tells me
that I could be another Shirley Strickland.
It is so good to have someone who believes in me.
I wish that he knew that most of the time I am scared.

Sheryl Carpenter

Did I hear you ask what I dream about?

I dream that one day I will have a pet – not a wild dog tied up by a chain.

I dream that one day I will come home from school and there will be enough afternoon tea for all of us – not just one or two pieces of bread for us to fight over.

I dream that one day my mum and dad will put down the plonk, remember about us kids and care enough to protect us.

I dream over, and over, and over again, that somehow, someone will hear me and get me to a safe place. I dream that someone will hear me and that no one will ever hurt me (or any other kid) ever again. That is what I dream about.

Did you hear me?

Did you hear my story?

You did?

Thank you.

I really needed to be heard.

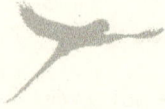

Many years have gone by since I was eleven. I have lived a full life. I have laughed a lot, shed tears, worked hard, played hard, met amazing people, and had the good fortune to do many things that my eleven-year-old self could not have even imagined.

I never got to be Australia's next Shirley Strickland, but I did get to represent a dear friend when he was inducted into the Australian Sports Hall of Fame. I am a mum, a grandma and a very good friend. I think I am a good human. Life is good.

Along the way, I have had but one wish. That wish is to somehow find the voice I didn't have as a child, and to use that voice to help others. It is my hope that in some small way, this book will do just that.

With love,

Sheryl

Hello... Can you hear me?